The Boston Dictionary

John Powers
illustrated by
Peter Wallace

Covered Bridge Press
North Attleborough, MA

TO PHIL —
YAW WIKKID PISSA, DUDE.

Peter Wallace

Covered Bridge Press
7 Adamsdale Road
N. Attleborough, MA 02760

!SBN 0-924771-85-2

10 9 8 7 6 5 4 3 2 1

ACKNOWLEDGMENTS

This Bawstin dictionary grew out of a shorter sampler which I wrote for the Boston Globe magazine in the winter of 1995. It provoked an enormous volume of mail and a phone call from Chuck Durang of Covered Bridge Press, who'd published a *Rhode Island Dictionary* by Mark Patinkin and Don Bousquet. He thought there might be a mahkit for a Bawstin version.

I owe sincere thanks to Chuck for his optimism and patience, to illustrator Peter Wallace for deftly putting these words into pickchiz, to Evelynne Kramer, my editor at the magazine who embraced the original bzah eyedeeyer, to the Globe for allowing me to use much of the sampler material in this volume and to the Pahwiz family, which provided me (wittingly or not) with a wealth of material.

HOW BAWSTIN TOKS

I never thought I talked with an accent. People from Noo Yawk and Jawja and Indianer talked with accents. I spoke English. Then I showed up at college with a broken nose and a black eye.

"What happened to you?" wondered my freshman roommate from Beverly Hills.

"Ran inta a pahked cah," I told him. He dashed off bewildered and came back with our other roommate from the Cleveland suburbs.

"Tell him what you just told me," he said.

Nobiddy awn owah dawm floah undastood me awl yeah. Guys from Brooklyn, from Wyoming, from Alabama scratched their heads and asked each other: What the hell is he saying?

People who ahnt bon heah think the Bawstin accent is bzah. But it's not hahd to masta. Just open your mouth and say "ah." Just like the docta tells you.

The Bawstin accent is merely the King's English (from East Anglia, actually), marinated in conned beef and cabbidj for a few centuries and doused with clam sauce from the Nawth End. It's based on the broad A and the dropped R, but most Americans (who say Basstun and Bahstin) can't mimic it to save their lives. Hollywood always gets it wrong. They have the guy from Bawstin sounding like Cliff Robertson imitating Jack Kennedy aboard PT 109. Or they give him a lockjaw, like Jeremy Irons doing Claus von Bulow. Or they have Cliff Clavin sounding retahded on "Cheers."

Bostonians don't talk like that. They talk like Mike Eruzione, the captain of the 1980 Olympic hockey team that beat the Soviets at Lake Placid. "Weah ahta heah, Donner," he told his girlfriend when a team party got a little rowdy for his taste. They talk like Jim Craig, the goalie who was searching for his Dad with the American flag around his neck asking: "Wayuh's my fahtha?"

Bostonians talk like Ernie Boch, the Route 1 auto salesman who offers "fawma leased cahs." They talk like Hizzonna the Mayah. They say "Hahwahya?" and "Shuah." They say yaw, yiz and yoz. They live in Dot and Rozzie and Southie and Eastie. They go up the State House and down the Cape. They put buddha on their con, they get cahdid at the packie, they have a sofer and a hassick in the pahla.

Bostonians take the Ahbuhway cah to the Emeffay to see the wotta culluz. They odda the veal pahm, pahster and Keeahntee at Tetchee's and buy ahmind krasonts and cawfee at O Bone Pan. They drink tonic and frappes and they shop at Jawdnz and Stah Mahkit. They go to Bee Cee and Bee Yew and Hahvid and Nawtheastin. They say 'Mutheragawd!' when they lose their khakis and hafta take the T to the Ianeah.

They follow the Broons, the Seltz, the Sawx and the Pats. They read Mike Bahnikul and watch Liz Wokka and listen to Howie Cah. Except for the Nawtheastiz in Febyooery, they think Bawstin is wikkid pissa. The one thing they don't do is pahk the cah in Hahvid Yahd.

A

A: Of. "Nuhpawnsit isn't a suburb. It's a paht a Dot."

AFTA: The owiz ahfta noon. "I figured ahd go to Coast Gahd beach this mawning but the sky is ovahcast. If it burns awf, I'll go this afta. Uhthawise, I'll go to the mawl."

AH: Are. "Ah yiz going upta Bah Hahba faw the Fowith?"

AHD: I would. "Ahd rahtha live in a cahdbowid box unda the ahdery than in a penthouse in Noo Yawk."

AHDERY: Elevated highway through downtown. "You know why they call it the ahdery? Because it's always clogged. At rush owah, it takes fotty minutes to go from Nawth Station to Chinertown. Cahs ah bumpa to bumpa fawevah."

AH FAHTHA: How the Lawd's Prayah stahts.

AHL: I will. "Ahl nevah fawget watching Cahltin Fisk's homa cleah the foul poewil."

AHM: Paht neah the sholda. "If Jim Lonbowuhg hadn't had a tyuhd ahm, he would've beaten the Cahds in the '67 Series." Also: I am.

AHNCHA: Are you not? "Yaw going to the Mahshfield Fayah, ahncha? I got a hoss running theyah."

AHNT: Sista of yaw fahtha aw mutha. "When Ahnt Mahther turned fotty lahst yeeah, we awl went to her pahty at Peeah Foah." Also: Ah not. "We ahnt goin' down the Cape tuhmawra becoz theyiz sposeta be a nawtheasta cummin."

AHSE: Backside. "Awsum play at the Paytreeuhts game lahst Sundee. Ben Coates nokked this Jaygwahz connaback ahse ovah teakettle."

AHSK: Inquire. "If you goda Tetchees, ahsk faw the steak ah lah Mahfeeyer. It's a speshul."

AHT: Pickchiz, etc. "My sista failed aht histaree at Weetin. She could nevah tell the Moanays apaht from the Mahnays."

AHM

AHTA: Out of. "My fayvrit Mehrull Streep puhfawmintz was Ahta Afriker."

ANSA: Response. "When that tourist from Iahland ahsked me wayuh South Dennis was, I couldn't give him an ansa. I mean, how do I tell him it's nawth of West Dennis?"

AW: Or. "Getting a job at Stah Mahkit isn't hahd. Awl you hafta know is hahda say 'Paypa aw plastic?' "

AWCHID: Wayuh payuhs grow. "If Mahther had grown peechiz instedda grapes, the Vinyid would be cawld the Awchid."

AWD: Kweea. "Visitiz to Bawstin find it awd to have baked beans faw brekfist."

AWDERVZ: Appuhtyziz. "Evah goda a tahpis bah? It's awl awdervz. You know, like sahdeenz."

AWF: Not awn. "You know what I nevah got about `Chahlie on the MTA'? Why doesn't his wife hand him a nickel instead of a sandwich as the trolley comes rumblin' through Scully Squayah station? Then the pooah bastid could get awf."

AWFIS: Wayuh workiz ah. "My fahthiz awfis awn Fedrul Street ovahlooks the Chahlz. On a cleeah day, you can see upta Hahvid."

AWLAYIZ: You (plural, inclusive). "When I said I could take yiz to Glosta, I didn't mean awlayiz. Ahv only got room faw foah in my Torris. Now, if I had the Voyija..."

AWN: Not awf. "So ahm in Noo Yawk, waiting to buy a ticket to the Broons-Raynjiz game and sumbiddy says, `Ah you awn line?'. I go, what is this, the Intanet? Ahm in line, not awn."

AWRINJ: Sitriss fruit. "Awl we got left faw tonic is awrinj soder and jinja."

AWSUM: Moah than impressive. "My fayvrit museum is the Peebiddy?? at Hahvid. Awl those glass flahwiz."

AYCAWN: Oak nut. "I always wundid why they cawl it aycawn squash. I mean, it doesn't grow on trees."

AYUH: Air. "If you wanta flyta Bufferlow from Bawstin, you hafta take Yew Ess Ayuh."

B

BAH: Serves beah and hahd likka. "The train to Noo Yawk takes foah owiz from South Station. Thank Gawd theyah's a bah cah."

BAHBA: A cutta of hayuh. "Sumbiddy wanted to know wayuh I get my hayuh cut. I told them I go to the Mayah's guy ovah in Hyde Pahk. Nine bucks faw a razuh cut and they throw in cawfee and cannolis. Why not that Safah guy on Newbree Street?, he asked me. Get real, I said. Fotty dolliz faw a bahba?"

BAHF: To regurgitate. "If I heah Achy Breaky Haht one moah time, ahm gonna bahf."

BAHTH: Hot wotta in a tub. "Most days, I only have time faw a shahwa. It takes hahf an owah faw a propah bahth."

BALD EAGLE: Bawstin Collidj alum (ovah fotty). "You know how you can tell a Bald Eagle? He's always tokking about Chahlie O'Roowik and the Shugah Bowl back befoah the waw."

BAWSTIN CREAM PIE: Frawstid layah cake. "If yaw evah at the Pahka House, ahsk faw the Bawstin cream pie. But you cahn't have it ah ler mode, because it's not a pie."

BAYAH: Ferocious brown mammal. "My dotta took this transfa student from Keenyer to the new Gahden to watch the Broons play the Stahz. What's a Broon, he says. You know, my dotta says. A bayah."

BEAH: Malt beverage. "Ahm down the Eerie Pub in Dotchesta and my fahtha tells me to odda him a beah. What kind, I ahsk him. I don't cayuh, he says. Hahp, Corohner, Koowiz. Anything but Cahling."

BAH

BEDDA: Should. "Yiz bedda staht faw the Cape now if yiz ah gunna make it to Awleenz faw suppa. Cahs ah backed upta Plimmith from the roedery."

BEE CEE: Bawstin Collidj. "You know how Bee Cee and Bee Yew ah ahch-rivals? Well, once you go westa Wista, everyone thinks theyah the same school."

BEE PEE ELL: Boston Public Library. "Ahm gunna hafta goda the Bee Pee Ell tuhmawra and scawa the ahkives faw those rekkids from the Guvna's Cownsil."

BEE YEW: Bawstin Yewniversiddy. "Wayuh ah you applying, sumbiddy ahsked me - Bee Cee aw Bee Yew? Bee Cee, I said. Bee Yew is awl Noo Yawkiz."

BAYAH

BLIZZID: Wikkid snowstawm. "The wetha says weah getting 12-to-16 tuhmawra. That's not a stawm. It's a freakin' blizzid."

BON: Brought into existence. "Whenevah people ahsk me what paht of Bawstin ahm from, I say I was bon in J.P. but brought up in Dot. What paht of Dot, they ahsk me? I say, neah Uppimz Conna."

BROODLE: Way hahsh. "I hadda wait an owah to get inta Zanzinbahz Satiddy night. Awl these Bee Yew sawfmoahs and oh payiz from Yoorip. Broodle."

BROONS: Professional hockey team, named ahfta bayahs. "I remembah back when Bobby Oah was playing, you hadda sell yaw mutha faw Broons tickets and they were up in the raftiz. Now, you can wok right in."

BUDDHA: Churned dairy product. "Some people cahn't have anything but mahjerin, but I hafta have my buddha, especially on baked puhdayduhs. Put it in chowda, melt it faw lobsta, spread it on krasonts. Ahl even use it on that fokahcher bread they give you at Pahpahrahtsee's."

HAHP LAHGA

BEAH

BULJAH: Fawma pawl. "Ahm out in Amherst and I see this guy in academic gahb, drinking a mokerchino and reading Eskyluss in the original. Turns out it's Billy Buljah, who yoosta run the state Sennit until the Guvna put him in chahj of UMass. Now, he's a skawla."

BREAD AND BUDDHA

BYUH: Purchisa. "My fahtha wanted to sell his triple decka on Dot Av down by Lowa Mills, but it sat on the mahkit faw a yeeah. Then he ran an ad saying it was neah Milton and he got a byuh in fotty-eight owiz."

THE BROONS

BZAH: Strange, odd. "Bawstin has wikkid bzah wehtha. One day, you'll have a blizzid, snow up to yaw ahse. The next day, it'll be so wawm you won't even need to wayuh a pahker."

C

CAHD: Plastic cash. "I wanted to buy a lonmowa at Seeyiz but I didn't have my chahj cahd and I was maxed out on Veezer. So I hadda go ovah to Leechmeah."

CHAHJ CAHD

CAHDID: To be required to produce identification. "I go down the packie lahst night faw a jug of Keeahntee and I get cahdid. This is unreal, I say to the guy. What do I look like, Alfalfer from Owah Gang?"

CAHDNAL: Ovahsees the ahchdiasis of Bawstin. "Memba when the Guvna pases out befoah giving a speech at Bentley and ends up in the hawspittle. He wakes up and sees this religious guy all gahbed in skahlit bending ovah him. I thought it was the Big Guy, the Guvna says. But it was only my friend the Cahdnal."

CAHN'T: Can not. "I cahn't go down the Vinyid tuhmawra because my sista got stawped faw dryvin unda with my Mahzder awn an expyuhd sticka. And my mota scoota needs a muffla."

CAWD: Bawstin's posta fish. "What's that fish up awn the Sennit wall faw? That's the saykrid cawd."

SAYKRID CAWD

HOLY MACKRIL

CAWF: Cough. "If you don't take cayah of that cawf, yaw gonna catch wokken nuhmoanya."

CAWFEE: Jahver. "I went inta Stahbucks this mawning and oddid a lahtay. Unreal. Three bucks faw a cuppa cawfee."

CAWMIN: Bawstin's back yahd. "Hahdaya tell the Cawmin apaht from the Public Gahden? You can graze yaw cattle awn the Cawmin."

CAWPRIT: Regahding bizniz. "Evah notice when the guvna toks about welfayah refawm, he's not tokken about cawprit welfayah?"

CAWRIDDA: Lawng hawl. "It's only been thirty yeeiz since they stahted the Southwest Cawridda. Otta be open any day now."

CAYUH: Give a damn. "Do you know who that is, says some guy in a bah. Mow Von, the Sawc slugga. Ahm like, ahsk me if I cayuh."

LAHJ CAWFEE

CHAHLIE: The man who nevah returned. "You know how they said he may ride fawevah 'neath the streets of Bawstin? If Chahlie's still unda theyah, it'll cost him 80 cents to get awf at Leechmeah now."

CHAHLZ: The rivah. "Me and my friend were trying to get into Daisy's on Newbree Street but he got cahdid and didn't have a license. What's yaw name, the bounsa goes. Chahlz Riviz, my friend says."

THE CAWMIN

CHATTUM: Chatham. "If yaw dryvin down 6 from P'town, go through Awleenz and keep awn until yaw undawotta. Then you'll know yaw in Chattum."

CHAWKLIT: Mahz bahz, etc. "My cuzzin lives down in Lowa Mills offa Dot Av. You know, neah Baykiz Chawklit."

CHAYUH: Foah-legged seat. "Woodja move that chayuh into the pahla nexta the sofer?"

CHOWDA: Clams, milk, buddha. "Sumbiddy offid me Manhattan-style chowda once. I said, only a Noo Yawka would put tuhmaydiz in chowda. Why not throw in a cheese Danish?"

CHUBLEE: Librul fyah wotta. "I hafta run out to Mahtinyeddi's faw Chublee and bree. Mike Dookahkis is coming ovah to tok about prizzin refawm."

CLOZ: Santer's lahst name. "Wayuh does Santer Cloz live, my dotta ahsked me. The Nawth Poewil, I said. Up theyah pahst Noo Hampsha." Also: lobsta hands.

COLLIDJ: Instatoot. "My dotta is going to Nawtheastin. That's not a direction. It's a collidj."

SANTER CLOZ

CON: Stahchy veggie that comes on a cob. "On Layba Day down the Vinyid, we have lobsta with dron buddha, puhdayduhs, con and beah."

CON AHTIST

CONNA: Wayuh streets meet. "Saying what paht of Bawstin yaw from isn't enough. Like if you live in Dot, you hafta say which conna. You know, Fields Conna, Uppimz Conna..."

CONSIT: Myoozikil puhfawmintz. "Didja heah what tickets faw the Mehtalliker consit ah going faw? Fotty dolliz. Unreal."

CUBBID: Used faw storridj. "I don't keep my Wottafid in the cubbid. I keep it in the chiner clawzit."

CULLUZ: Heeyooz. "My nayba had her culluz done at Culla Me Beeyewdiful. She's a winta. You know, chahcoal, skahlit, teeyul."

CUZZIN: Son aw dotta of yaw ahnt aw unkil. "How small is Chahlztown? Well, everyone theyah is my sekkind cuzzin."

CONSIT

ONLY IN BAWSTIN

Boston cream pie: Bostonians almost never make it at home, but it's unavoidable at college dining halls and company cafeterias. It may be shaped like a pie and it's served in wedges, but it's a yellow layer cake with boiled cream in the middle and chocolate frosting on top. It's served chilled, so you can stick leftovers in the fridge and serve them again days - or weeks - later. Some upscale restaurants will tart it up with slivered almonds or splash a jigger of rum in the cream, but the basics haven't changed since the 19th century.

Cardinal: Since there's only one (and Boston has had one almost since the Sermon on the Mount), he's always referred to with the definite article: The Cardinal. When they're being formal they'll call him Bernard Cardinal Law, but that's considered unnecessary. When Richard Cushing was Cardinal, his nasal drawl was so distinctive that every Bostonian could identify him by voice alone.

Chowder: Ishmael sampled it in "Moby Dick" and it's served at Fenway Park. It's a blend of milk, butter, seafood, and seasonings, but how it's made isn't as important as how much fish is in it. Clam chowder should have big chunks of chopped quahaugs (pronounced co-hawgs), the big chewy clams that aren't as palatable whole. Fish chowder is catch-of-the-day stuff. Bostonians will even eat corn chowder, but usually out of a can. Most places will also put potatoes and onions in their chowder, especially if they're serving it to tourists. But if there are tomatoes in it (i.e. Manhattan-style), it isn't chowder. It's a Noo Yawk nightmayah.

D

DAHK: Awpasit of light. "My fayvrit candy bah was Fawreva Yoz. Awl that dahk chawklit."

DANVIZ: Danvers. "If the Libidy Tree was in Bawstin, how come the Libidy Tree Mawl is in Danviz? That's awl the way up in the Nawth Shoah."

DAPPA: Counsila O'Neil. "So I go inta Wottaminz and who do I see at the casket, saying the Ah Fahtha? Dappa. He was unahmed, though. Left his revolva at the doah."

DAWG: Canine. "Sumbiddy wanted to know hahda get to Wundaland to see the dawgs run. I said, take the Blue Line to Reveah and wok until you heah bahking."

DAWM: Collidj residence. "My bruthiz dawm at Nawtheastin is kitty-conna from Jawdn Hawl."

DEDDUM: Dedham. "This lawst guy ahsked me wayuh Dead Ham was. All ham is dead, I infawm him. Then I figya out he means Deddum. It's neah heah, I go. Between Needum and Hyde Pahk."

DOCTA: Physician, academic, etc. "At Bee Yew, you're sposeta address the president as Docta Silba. I don't know what he's a docta of, but I bet he's nevah been around a cadavah."

DOE-UH: What you shut. "Owah sella doe-uh is awf kilta. Weah gunna hafta hyah a cahpinta."

DOLLIZ: Greenbacks. "You know what they want faw two Broons seats this yeah? Ninedy dolliz. Faw that, Bobby Oah otta make me dinna."

DOT: Shot faw Dotchesta. "When I say I grew up in Dot, people always ahsk me if I know Mahky Mahk. I say, well, Dot is wikkid lahj. He was from St. William's, I was from St. Greg's. So Mahky might as well have been on Mahz."

DOTTA: Female child. "Was that yaw dotta playing Clahra in the Nutcracka? She was wikkid awsum."

DROZ: Dressa compahtments. "I cahn't get any moah cloze in my droz. Theyah fulla winta swettiz." Also: undawayah.

DRYVIZ: Cah ohniz. "I don't know why everyone says Bawstin dryviz ah so crazy. Evah see a Noo Yawka inside a roedaree? Looks like Uhpawlo 13 in awbit."

E

EAH: What you heah with. "If you wayuh awrinj ta the St. Paddy's Day puhrayd in Southie, they'll tawss you out awn yaw eah."

EASTA: Paschal feast. "When we go to Saykrid Haht faw Easta, they always have awkids on the alta."

EMEFFAY: The Museum of Fine Ahts. "Ah yiz goin' to the Emeffay faw the Renwa exhibit? Awsum wotta culluz. Too hahd to pahk theyah, though. Bedda take the trolley and get awf at the green Indian on the hoss."

ESS JAY CEE: Supreme Judicial Court. "I ahsked this loya I know if he'd evah wanna be on the Ess Jay Cee. He said he'd hafta take the vow of pawviddy."

EVACUATION DAY: When the Redcoats took off. "When I went down to City Hall to pay my pahking tickets on Mahch 17th, the place was closed. I said, I know the Irish ah in chahj around heah, but taking St. Patrick's Day awf? Then somebody told me it was Evacuation Day. No wunda nobiddy was theyah."

EMEFFAY

EYEDEEYER: Brainstawm. "I wunda whose eyedeeyer it was to build Lowgin awn the wotta. Whenevah theyiz a blizzid, you need a dogsled to get ahta theyah."

EYE IN: Hahd grey mettil. "Kevin McHale, who yoosta play faw the Seltz, came from the Eye In Range in Minnersoter, up neah Canader."

EYEL'IND: Surrounded by wotta. "You shuhda been on Nantuckit when Hurricane Edwahd hit lahst summa, with evrybuddy trying to get offa the eyelind at once. It was like the fawl of Sighgawn."

F

FAH: Not neah. "The new guy at work wants to know hahda get to the Nawth End from the South End. Well, it's too fah to wok, I tell him. You'll get lawst driving and taking the T is too bzah. You just cahn't get theyah from heah."

FAHMIZ: Krawp rayziz. "The Fahmiz Almanac says weah infaw a rekkid winta faw snow. If it's moah than lahst yeah, ahm moving to Juhmaker."

FAW: On behahf of. "Evah heah the Bee Cee almer mahta? It's cawld 'Faw Bawstin.' "

FAWFIT: To hand ovah. "If owah sokka team cahn't find foah moah playiz, weah gunna hafta fawfit owah openah tuhmawra in Rozzie."

FAWK: Eating utensil. "When you go to the No-Name Restaurant down the Fish Peeah, they give you two fawks faw the lobsta. The smalla one is faw the cloz."

FAWMA: Yoosta be. "See that shot guy with the dahk eyebrows on the Rivahside trolley cah? That's Mike Dookahkis, the fawma guvna."

FAWRINNUZ: Not from heah. "You can always tell who the fawrinnuz ah in Bawstin. They tryda tok to us in English."

FAWMA GUVNA

FAYAH: What life isn't. "It's not fayah that in Masserchoosits we hafta pay income tax, inheritance tax, prawpitty tax, sales tax, meals tax - even auto excise tax. Up in Noo Hampsha, it's `Live Free Aw Die'. Okay, so theyah guvna's a raccoon."

FEBYOOERY: Befoah Mahch. "We don't have snowstawms in Bawstin in Febyooery. We have blizzids."

FETHIZ: Bird cuvviz. "Nobiddy's used tah and fethiz in Bawstin since the Sunsalibidy."

FLAHWIZ: Awkids, puhtoonyuz, etc. "It isn't hahd to tell the Commin apaht from the Public Gahden. The Gahden's the one with flahwiz and frawgz."

FLAWRIDDER: Jawja with sand and miskeetiz. "My inloz sold theyah triple decka in Rozzie and moved into a campa in Flawridder. They said they were traydin up."

FLOAH: What you wok on. "Is Room Foah Fotty Foah on the fowith aw the fotty fowith floah?"

FOAH: One moah than three. "Whenevah I heah sumbiddy say `Foah moah yeeiz', I cahn't help thinking of Richid Nicksin."

FOKAHCHER: Bread from Flawrintz. "The guy nexta me at Fuhleesher's sent back the bread because it was stale. That's not bread, the wayda told him. That's fokahcher."

FOT: Engaged in ahmed cawnflict. "Mem Drive is named faw the soldjiz who fot in the waw."

FOTTY: Foah times ten. "I couldn't believe when they stahted chahjin fotty dolliz to see the Seltz. I mean, I coulda bot the Gahden faw that."

FOWIDZ: Towidz the front. "Some people cahn't figya out Dotchesta. But I know it fowidz and backwidz."

FRAPPE: Milk, ice cream and syrup blended together. "My cuzzin from Iower ahsked the Brigumz guy faw a chawklit milk shake. If you want ice cream in it, I told him, odda a frappe."

FYAH: Oxygen and a spahk. "The ahdery was backed up pahst Chahlztown because of a cah fyah neah Rowes Wof."

FYUSHA: Goddy culla. "Hahda you describe fyusha? It's skahlit and lavenda mooshed togetha."

NAYBAHOODS

Bawstin is a city of "naybahoods." Saying you're from Boston is like saying you're from Los Angeles. "What paht?," the Bostonian will ask you. Eastie? Southie? Dot? Rozzie? The naybahoods are broken down into "conniz" and "skwayiz"—e.g. Uppimz Conna, Yoonyun Skwayah. "Ahm from Melville Pahk," a Dot boy will say. "Between Codmin Skwayah and Fields Conna."

PAHTS A BAWSTIN

Dot = Dorchester
Eastie = East Boston
J.P. = Jamaica Plain
Rozzie = Roslindale
Southie = South Boston

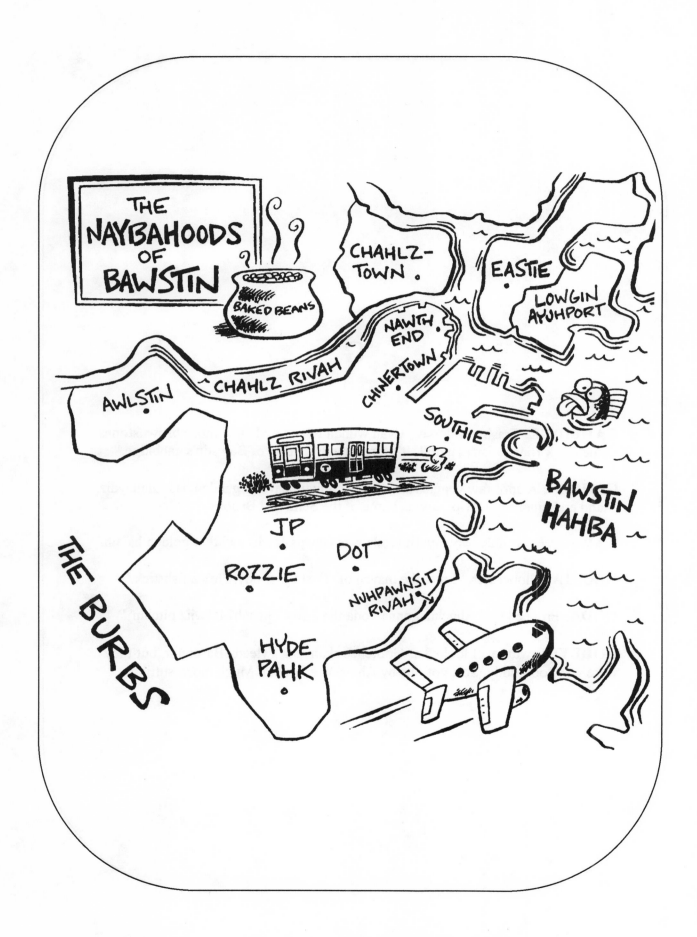

G

GAHBIDGE: Trash, swill, etc. "Evah wunda what's unda awl those brownstones in the Back Bay? It isn't landfill. It's three hundrid yeeiz of Bawstin's gahbidge."

GAHDEN: A spot faw veggies and flowiz. "Owuh nayba's gahden has tuhmaydiz, chahd and zinniyuz." Also: fawma home of the Seltz and Broons.

GAWJIS: Beautiful. "My fayvrit ressla was Gawjis Jawj - awl that golden hayuh."

GLOSTA: Gloucester. "I met the mayah of Glosta yestiddy. He's a fishstick."

GODA: Proceed to. "Ahnchiz gonna goda the Sawx openah? Rawjiz pitchin'."

GODDY: Tawdree. "I looked at Gootchee skahvz at Fyleenz Basemint, but they were way too goddy. So I got one by Ahmahnee instead. Much moah suttil."

GUNNA: Going to. "Ah yiz gunna go upta Dahtmith faw the Winta Cahnivul in Febyooery? Theyah sposeta have a pissa bawnfyah."

GUVNA: Chief executive of the commonwealth. "Ahm wokken down Pahk Street on my lunch owah and this tall Yankee with awrinj hayah and a squash rackit goes by. It's the guvna, awn his way to cut moah taxes."

H

HADDA: Was required to. "I hadda goda the bahbiz yestiddy. My hayah was a dizasta."

HAFTA: Must. "I hafta goda Lemminsta this afta faw a shahwa."

HAHBA: Site of the Bawstin Tea Pahty. "I was eating a veal pahm sub in Kwinzee Mahket when this guy from Ahjentiner ahsked me wayuh the hahba was. Simple, I go. Just wok east 'til yaw hat floats."

HAHBA TAHWIZ: Wottafront Tahj Muhahl. "You know how Noo Yawk has the Statchew of Libidy faw a landmahk? In Bawstin, we have Hahba Tahwiz."

HAHD: Difficult. "Theyah's an awsum line in one of Jawj Higgins' books about Bawstin. Guy says, it's a hahd life, but it's hahda if yaw stoopid."

HAHDA: How to. "Best way hahda make conned beef and cabbidge is the way my Nanner yoosta. Covah everything with wotta and boil it until the meat turns gray and the cabbidge falls apaht." Also: moah hahd.

HAHDLY: Neahly nawt. "You can hahdly find anyone who makes Indian pudding any moah."

HAHF-AHST: Done without regahd faw detail. "Evah wundah why Bawstin's streets ah so weeuhd? Because they yoosta be cow pahths leading to the Commin. What a hahf-ahst way to lay out a city."

THIS IS HAHF AHST!

CAUTION COWS WORKING

HAHLAKWIN: A blend of vanilla, chocolate and strawberry ice creams. "I was going crazy about what to serve at my dotta's birthday pahty. You know how finicky foah-yeeah-olds ah. Buddha peekahn? Pistahsheo? Nah, my nayba says. Just give 'em awl hahlakwin."

HAHPAHST: Thirty minutes ahfta the owah. "My ahnt ahsked me when the Sox game would be ovah. I said hahpahst foah, unless Rawja is pitchin."

HAHT: Muskyoola awgin. "My grand-ahnt from Flawridder ahsked me if I would take her to Jawdnz when she comes up faw Easta. I didn't have the haht to tell her it's been taken ovah by Noo Yokkiz."

HAHVID: Country day school across the rivah. "This guy in Kenmoah Skwayah ahsks me how to get to Hahvid. Bedda be a Merit Skawla, I say. Aw change yaw name to Cabbit."

HAHWAHYA: How are you? "Ahm down at Doyle's, you know, the bah in J.P., and who do I run into but Raybo, the fawma mayah. He says: Hahwahya, Ahtha, have a Hahp lahga. And how about those Seltz?"

HAWSPITTLE: Bawstin City, etc. "My bruthiz an oddaly at Mass Genrull. That's the hawspittle down by the Chahlz wayuh the Ianeah is."

HAYUH: Tresses. "Yaw from Meffa, right, some guy on the Awrinj Line says. Hahdidja know, I go. Yaw hayuh, he says. It's so lahj."

LAHJ HAYUH

HEAH: Done with the eahs. "Listen my children and yiz shall heah of the midnight ride of Pawl Reveah." Also: not theyah. "The Emeffay isn't fah from heah by trolley. Just take the Ahbuhway cah from Pahk."

HOSS: Equine quadruped. "We took Nanner ovah to Suffick Downs faw some fresh ayuh and she bets her Social Security check on this $200 clayma. She's at the toppa the stretch with her wokka goin', 'C'mon, Foah Hoss!' Ends up hitting the puhfekter faw six grand. Bedda than the lawdery."

I

IANEAH: The Eye and Ear Infirmary at Mass. General Hospital. "Nanner couldn't heah the howitzas at the end of the 1812 Ovitcha at the Esplinahd. So we took her down the Ianeah."

INDOWIZ: Not outdowiz. "Lahst yeah we hadda move owah Layba Day bahbikyew indowiz awn accounta the stawm. So I grilled the sawsijiz on skeeooiz in the fyahplace."

INFAWM: Apprise. "When was the Bawstin Massika, owah histaree teecha ahsks me. 1978, I infawm her. That's when the Yankees nokked in 42 runs at Fenway and beat the Sawx foah straight."

INJID: Hahmd. "If Bobby Oah hadn't injid his knees, the Broons wooda won a coupla moah Stanley Cups faw shuah."

ONLY IN BAWSTIN, PAHT II

Dot: If you'd uttered the word "Dorchester" a few thousand times, you'd shorten it to Dot, too. It's Dot because the Bostonian pronounces it "Dotchesta." Thus: Dot Av, Dot High, Dot Park. Dorchester is so huge that saying you're from Dot doesn't mean anything. You have to specify what "paht," either by neighborhood (e.g. Neponset, Uphams Corner, Codman Square, Savin Hill) or by parish (St. Mark's, St. William's, St. Gregory's, St. Brendan's, St. Peter's, St. Ambrose's, St. Ann's).

Esplanade: Just try to find it on a map, or to get directions if you pronounce it as it's spelled. It's the "Esplinahd," the grassy stretch along the Charles basin where the Back Bay rubs up against Beacon Hill. The Boston Pops gives its free summer concerts at the Hatch Shell on the Esplanade. The big one comes on July 4, highlighted by Tchaikovsky's "1812 Overture," complete with howitzer fire and pyrotechnics.

Evacuation Day: Boston's most parochial holiday, it's celebrated on March 17 to commemorate the day the British decided to leave the city during the Revolutionary War. Nobody remembers why they left (Yankee cannons pointing down on them from Dorchester Heights were a prime reason) or where they went. But as far as Bostonians were concerned, the war was over when the redcoats vanished. If you work in the city (and for the city), you get the day off. Since it's also St. Patrick's Day, you get an excuse to drink.

Frappe: Everybody else in America calls it a milk shake (okay, in Rhode Island it's a cabinet). In Boston, it's a frappe. Not a "frap-pay," as the French call it. A "frap." If you order a milk shake, you'll get just the milk and the syrup without the ice cream.

J

JAWDNZ: Depahtment stoah. "I got a chahj cahd in the mail from Macy's. You know, the New Yawk stoah that took ovah Jawdn Mahsh. I don't cayuh whatcha call it, it'll always be Jawdnz to me."

JAWJA: Alabamer's nayba. "What did Shermin do ahfta he mahched through Jawja? Goda the beach?"

JINJA: Tangy twisted herb. "I go to this new beestro in the South End and odda a rye and jinja. We don't have any rye, the wayda says. But you can have the jinja on a krassont with some alfalfer sprouts."

J.P.: Jamaica Plain. "Pahking in J.P. isn't so hahd. Finding it is the prawblm."

JOONYA: Not seenya. "Memba that Alabamer football playuh cawld E.J. Joonya? He was so lahj, I wooda hated to run inta E. J. Seenya."

K

KEEAHNTEE: Tuscan grape juice. "What goes bedda with veal pahm and pahster than Keeahntee?"

KHAKIS: What you staht the cah with. "We were already hahf an owah late faw the Mahky Mahk consit when my sista said she'd lost her khakis. Ahm like, this is so retahded."

KONKID: Concord. "I nevah undastood why the British mahched out to Konkid in the first place. Awl they had out theyah was awchidz."

KOT: Hooked. "When was that mackril kot? Smells like lahst yeah."

KRASONT: French turnovah. "Evah odda the Irish krasont at O Bone Pan? They put conned beef and cabbidge inside."

KRULLA: Awblawng doenit. "If yaw going out to Dunkin Doenitz, get me a krulla and a lahj cawfee with kreema and foah shugiz."

KWEEA: Silly, retahded. "My mutha told me I have to wayuh my sista's jumpa from lahst yeeah. I said, no way. This is so kweea."

KWOTTA: One-fowith. "So, when should I meetcha? How about kwotta ahfta the owah at the conna of Dahtmith and Comm Av?" Also: 25 cents.

KWYA: Sunday singiz. "Owah nayba sings tenna faw the ahchdyossissin kwya. When he does the Ahvay Muhreeyer, you'd swayah he was the Ahkaynjil Gaybreeyul."

KWOTTA

L

LAD'N: Jawn Hancock's almer mahta. "The hahdest paht about Lad'n School isn't getting in. It's getting out."

LAHF: Chortle, guffaw. "I heard some guy from Arazoner trying to imitate owah accent. `Pack the caa', he was saying. You nevah lahfed so hahd."

LAHJ: Ovahsized. "Whenevah I go to Dunkin' Doenitz, I always odda a krulla and a lahj cawfee with shugah."

LAHTAY: Italian au lait. "You can chahj a dolla moah faw cawfee with milk if you just cawl it a lahtay."

LAWD: The saveya. "My ahnt as bon in Glosta in the yeah of Ah Lawd Nineteen Fotty-Foah."

LAWDERY: Game of chance. "Sumbiddy ahsked me if I evah play the lawdery. I said, well, I jaywok in Hahvid Skwayah."

LAYBA: Work. "I was gonna go down the Cape faw Layba Day, but they say the backup from the Bon Bridge is unreal."

LAYDA: Not now. "If you live in Bawstin long enough, soona aw layda you staht tokking like the mayah."

LIKKA: An alcoholic beverage. "What've you got faw likka faw the christening, I ahsked my brutha. You mean beah - or hahd stuff, he told me. Hahd stuff, I said. You know, vodker, Bacahdi, berbin. The packie closes in hahf an owah. If you don't hurry, we'll be drinking Bally ale and the communion wine."

LOFIZ: Weejuns, etc. "Lofiz with no sawx? Wayuh do you think you ah? Nantuckit?"

LONMOWA: Grass cutta. "My naybiz new lonmowa looks moah like a Jawn Deeah tracta."

LOYA: An attorney. "I saw by the paypa that his nibs from Meffa got named a Superiya Cowit justice lahst week. Like they say, a judge is just a loya who knew a guvnah."

TOWNS AROUND BAWSTIN

If a Bostonian tells you that you "cahn't get theyah from heah," you're probably mispronouncing your destination. Which is to say, you're probably saying it the way it's spelled. TV anchorpersons, imported from Middle America last month, do it all the time. "Meanwhile, in Stuffton..." they say. Or Hayverhill. Or Woosta.

Bostonians have never heard of those places. But they can direct you to Stoetin and Hayvril, Wista and Glosta, Meffa and Chemzfid. A glossary of Grayta Bawstin and beyond:

Awbin = Auburn	Hahvid = Harvard
Awleenz = Orleans	Hayvril = Haverhill
Ayuh = Ayer	Hingum = Hingham
Birricka = Billerica	Konkid = Concord
Cahva = Carver	Kwinzee = Quincy
Chattum = Chatham	Lemminsta = Leominster
Chemzfid = Chelmsford	Linkin = Lincoln
Danviz = Danvers	Lole = Lowell
Deddum = Dedham	Mahlbro = Marlborough
Draykit = Dracut	Mahthiz Vinyid = Martha's Vineyard
Evrit = Everett	Meffa = Medford
Frayminham = Framingham	Nawfick = Norfolk
Glosta = Gloucester	Nawth Redding = North Reading
Grawtin = Groton	Nawtin = Norton

Needum = Needham
Pahma = Palmer
Peebidee = Peabody
P'town = Provincetown
Reveah = Revere
Sawgis = Saugus
Sitchooit = Scituate

Stoetin = Stoughton
Tontin = Taunton
Wayuh = Ware
Wennum = Wenham
Wista = Worcester
Woobin = Woburn
Wottatown = Watertown

Yahmith = Yarmouth

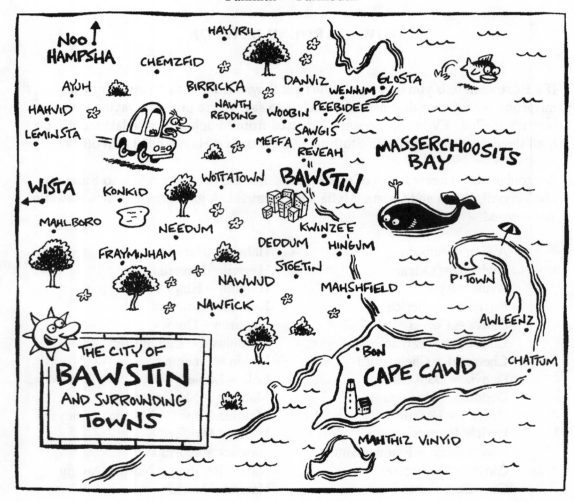

M

MAHKIT: Food stoah. "I hafta go back to the mahkit. I fawgawt mahshmelliz faw the sweet puhdaydiz."

MAHZ: Skahlit plannit. "I didn't find it awd that they discuvvid signs of life on Mahz. I mean, wayuh did they think the Mahz bah came from?"

MASSERCHOOSITS: State of kayoss. "They cahn't call it Taxerchoosits any moah since the guvna got ridda taxes. Awl we have in Masserchoosits now ah revenyoo enhancements."

MAYAH: Chief executive of the city. "Ahm awn the Fawrist Hills bus going down Hyde Pahk Av and who's standing on the conna yelling into a cah phone but Tommy Maneeno. Sumbiddy fawgawt to pick up the gahbidge and the mayah's all pissed awf. "This is a high-numbid wod," Tommy's going. "Theyah yoosta services heah."

MAYJA: Not myna. "Owah sella was so fulla wotta ahfta that broodle Nawtheasta, we hadda have majya reepayiz to owah burna."

MEFFA: Medford. "Guy in a cah in Reveeah ahsks hahda goda Medford. Nevah heard of it, I say. It's sposeta be neah heah, he says. Oh, I go, you mean Meffa."

MOAH: Grayta. "If yiz have any moah peetser, yaw stummicks will bust apaht like an ovah-filled tyuh."

MOTTLE: Causing eternal damnation. "My grandfahtha told me he hadda goda Bee Cee because it wooda been a mottle sin to goda Hahvid with awl those Prawdistints."

MUHNOOA: Bovine or equine fertilizer. "I ahsked owah nayba why his roses ah redda than myin. "It's awl in the hoss muhnooa," he infawmed me.

MUTHERAGAWD!: Favored expletive of a fawma mayah. "Ahm wokken down the cawridda at Bee Yew and I heah sumbiddy go:

MAYAH MANEENO

`Mutheragawd!' I know it's not Silba. Shuah enough, it's Kevin White. You know, the mayah befoah Raybo. He's a professa theyah."

MYIN: Not yoz. "I think that fyusha seeahsuckah jackit is myin. Yoz is way too shot faw my ahms."

N

NANNER: Yaw fathiz mutha. "Nanner is a mayja histawrikul figya. She saw the Sawx win the 1918 Series."

NAWTH: Above south. "When I tell people ahm from Bawstin, they ahsk me how I can live so fah nawth. Bawstin's in the East, I say. Noo Hampsha and Nover Skoesher ah nawth."

NAWTHEASTA: A multi-day stawm that comes awf the wotta. "When it rains yestiddy, tudday and tuhmawra in Bawstin, it's a Nawtheasta. When it happens in Febyooery, we call it a blizzid."

NAWTHEASTIN: Trolley collidj. "Best way to get to Nawtheastin is to take the Ahbuhway cah from Pahk and get awf ahfta the tunnel. If you see the Emeffay, you've gone too fah."

NAYBA: Lives next dowa. "My nayba moved heah from Califawniya. He'd nevah seen snow befoah, much less a blizzid."

N.I.N.A.: No Irish Need Apply. "Back befoah Honey Fitz was mayah, stoahs all ovah Bawstin had these N.I.N.A. signs in the windiz, put theyah by the Yankees. If

NAYBAS

you were bon in Wottafid aw Claya, you hadda be a hod carriya aw a streetcah conducta."

NOO HAMPSHA: Lahj campsite. "Hahda you get to Noo Hampsha? Go nawth 'til you see a toll booth and a likka stoah."

NOO YAWK: Ahmpit of Ameriker, 240 miles south of Tremont Street. "My friend from L.A. wanted to know what's all this tok about the Curse of the Bambino. I said, it's why the Sawx cahn't win the Series, evah since they sold Babe Ruth to Noo Yawk."

NUHMOANYA: Lung prawblm. "If you don't wayah that pahker on First Night, yaw gonna get wokken nuhmoanya."

I HEAH THEYAH'S A NAWTHEASTA COMING.!

OWAH: Sixty minutes. "Evah try to get from Rozzie to Eastie by cah? Even if the tunnel isn't jammed, it'll take you an owah. Theyah ahnt any shot cuts." Also: belonging to us. "When Noo Yawkiz complain about owah wotta, I ahsk them why they all drink Eveeahn." Also: belonging to us.

O

OAH: Greatest Broon evah. "Every time I wok pahst the Gahden, I can still heah Frank Fallon, the old announsa, going: 'Bawstin goal by Numbah Foah - Oah.' " Also: what the Hahvid crew rows with.

ODDA: Dining request. "We're at Jimmy's lahst night and the waitress comes up and says: Ahm Mahther, can I take yiz odda? Shuah, I say. Steemiz and beah to staht, then a two-poundah with a small Seeza."

OFFA: Adjacent to. "Nanner yoosta live off Senta Street in J.P. befoah she moved to Flawridda."

ONNIZ: Lawrilz. "My dotta graduated mahgner from Lahfeeyett. That's with high onniz."

OTTER: Should. "Yiz otter put a Diehahd in yaw Voyija befoah winta."

OVITCHA: Awkestrul staht. "Pahking was so hahd neah the Wang faw Fantim of the Oprah that we wokked in hahfway through the ovitcha."

P

PACKIE: A likka stoah. "It was so wawm yestiddy that we wanted something refreshing but taht. You know, like a Cape Codda. But we were ahta vodker, so I hadda run down the packie. The guy wants foahteen dolliz faw Smirnoff. I said, hey, ahm not buying faw the Zah heah. He says, so go to Mahtinyeddi's."

PAHK: Stop a cah. "Anytime people heah ahm from Bawstin, they go: Say pahk yaw cah in Hahvid Yahd. And ahm like, you cahn't pahk theyah. You'll get towed to Meffa."

PAHKA: Someone who pahks a cah. "My friend Jawj is a valet at Grill 23 on Berklee Street. You know, a cah pahka."

PAHKAY: Wooden floah. "People say it was the mystique that won the Seltz awl those world titles. I say it was the pahkay. The Seltz knew wayuh the dead spots were." Also: mahjerin.

PAHKER: What you wayah in the winta. "When I heard a blizzid might be cummin, I went to Jawdnz and put a pissa pahker on my chahge cahd. Only fotty dolliz mahked down."

ONLY IN BAWSTIN, PAHT III

Harvard: Want to pick out the Bostonian from a crowd with one word? Have him pronounce the school across the river. It's "Hahvid." Not "Hahvahd," as the T-shirts proclaim. Not "Havvid," as Bobby Kennedy would say. The spelling has nothing to do it. There's no R in Hahvid, just as there's no O in Bawstin.

Ianeah: If you live in the city long enough, you'll end up at Mass. General's Eye and Ear Infirmary. Bostonians call it the Ianeah, but it handles the nose and throat, too. The night Red Sox outfielder Tony Conigliaro was hit in the eye with a fastball (virtually ending his career), he was taken, spikes and all, to the Ianeah.

Jordan's: Macy's took over Jordan Marsh and changed the name, but Bostonians think of it—and some still call it Jordan's. It was one of the city's grand 19th-century department stores along Washington Street, spitting distance from rival Filene's, whose basement was decidedly more famous than what was above it. Every baby boomer in the area went there as a child during Christmas season to see the Enchanted Village and most ended up getting charge cards - their introduction to the endless joys of revolving credit.

Northeaster: A nasty storm borne off the ocean by the northeast wind. It lasts for the better part of two days and prompts everyone to stock up on milk, bread, water, AA batteries, candles and videos. The Blizzard of '78 was a Northeaster. You'll see it spelled Nor'easter in the newspapers, but most Bostonians won't pronounce it that way. They'll call it a Nawtheasta and curse it for days before and after.

PEAH FOAH: Restaurant ovahlooking the Hahba. "You'll never guess who I ran inta at Chahlie Flariddy's time at Peah Foah. Dappa himself. I said, Counsila O'Neil, if you have one moah pawpovah, you'll bahf."

PEEKAHN: Atlanter nut. "Brigumz was ahta Heath bah so we oddid buddha peekahn."

PIAZZER: Front porch. "When we lived in the triple decka awn Dot Av, all the naybiz sat out on the piazzer ahfta suppa."

PICKCHIZ: Moner Liser, et al. "This woman comes up outside the Isabeller Stewit Gahdna and ahsks wayuh the Jawn Singa Sahjent pickchiz ah. You want the Emeffay, I tell her. Ovah theyah, awn the uhtha side of the Fens."

PAHLA: Wayuh the sofer and hassick ah. "Ahfta dinna, we awl went in the pahlah faw cawfee and Sambuker. Uhtha places have living rooms. In Bawstin, we have pahliz."

PAHM: Breaded and fried cutlet. "Whenevah I go to Tetchees down the Nawth End, I odda the veal pahm with paster. So tenda you can cut it with a fawk."

PAHSELZ: Coach of the professional football team neah Pawtucket. "Whattaya think of the tuner, some guy in a bah goes? If you cahn't fry it, I say, it's not a fish. Naw, he says, I mean the Tuner. You know, Pahselz."

PAHSTER: Spaghetti, ziti, etc. Comes with veal pahm. "I nevah odda just pahster when I go to Mahmer Mariuz. Awla the main dishes come with pahster anyway."

PAHT: Naybahood of Bawstin. "What paht a Bawstin ah you from? J.P.? Ahm from Dot, down by Fields Conna. I was an alta boy at St. Mahk's."

PAHTY: A social gathering. "I got an invitation to a pahty faw the guvna at the Hahvid Club on Comm Av. Fotty dolliz faw awdervz and Chublee. That's not a pahty, I said. That's a time."

PASTA: Rectah of a parish. "Monseenya Gahvey yoosta be the pasta ovah to St. Mahgritz offa Dot Ave. Then the Cahdnal sent him to Saykrid Haht in Rozzie."

PAWL: Public servant, e.g. mayah. "I still cahn't believe that Ray Flynn is Vadikkin ambassida, ovah theyah with Jawn Pawl Two. Not bad faw a Southie pawl."

PAWVIDDY: Indigence. "Memba when Ell Bee Jay declayid the Waw Awn Pawviddy? Well, I think the pooah won."

PAYPA: News journal. "The old Yankees always said the only two times you want yaw name in the paypa is when yaw bon and when you die."

PISSA: Superb, sublime. "If you go to Dawginz on St. Paddy's Day, they give you a pissa dinna - soder bread, conned beef and cabbidge, boiled puhdaydiz, a bawl and a beah and Bawstin cream pie."

PITCHIZ: Hurliz of hosshides. "Weah ahguing about pitchiz and we get to the 1975 Series, which we figya the Sox had nokked ahfta Cahlton hits the homa. And all of us still agree: Zimma nevah shoulda taken out Willuhbee."

PLAHZER: Public prawmenahd. "Finding City Hawl Plahzer isn't a prawblm, even faw fawrinnuz. It's aykiz of bricks, just like Red Skwayah. Awl that's missing is the Kremlin tahwiz."

POOAH: Unrich. "Ahm going down Congress Street and this tourist from Indianer or Iderho ahsks me about the two statues of the shot guy across from the Purple Shamrock theyah. That's James Michael Curley, I infawm him. Mayah of the Pooah."

PEAH FOAH

POWICK: Sholda, baykin, etc. "Hahdaya know if yaw eating Bawstin baked beans? When theyiz salt powick and unyinz inside."

PRAWPITTY: What owniz have. "My nayba is in chahj of Real Prawpitty faw the city. Who's in chahj of Unreal Prawpitty? You know, like the Meggerplex?"

PRIZZIN: Jayul. "This guy told me he just moved to Nawfick. That's not a town, I said. That's a prizzin. You know, like Wallpoewil."

PSDS: Lobes with holes. "My sista went down to Kwinzee Mahkit yestiddy and came back with a pullovah swetta and PSDS."

PSDS

MR. PUHDAYDUH HEAD

P'TOWN: Provincetown. "Hahdaya know yaw in P'town? When the guys have PSDS."

PUHDAYDUH: Irish vegetable. "The wife and I went to the Hilltop up in Sawgis and oddid the Noo Yawk strip rayuh. Want peelahf with that, the girl wants to know. Naw, I go, just bring me a baked puhdayduh."

PYOOTA: Hahdly silva. "Did they use a silva aw pyoota servis at the Bawstin Tea Pahty? Only Pawl Reveah knows faw shuah."

Q

See "K"

R

RAWJA: Mr. Clemens. "I still remember bein' in the bleechiz the night Rawja struck out 20 Mariniz. Sumbiddy just kept hangin' K cahds up awn the wall theyah."

RECKA: Tow truck. "Foah-cah pileup on the Juhmakerway during rush owah tudday. They hadda bring a fyah truck, a coupla ambyoolintzis and a recka."

RETAHDED: Stupid, silly. "So my fahtha shows up in his Ahmahni blayza, shots and lofiz. We're going to dinna in P'town, I remind him. Yaw gonna look retahded."

REVEAH: Paytriyit, silvahsmith. "You know how Pawl Reveah wokked through the Nawth End, took a boat across the hahba and rode a hoss through every Middlesex city and town, shouting `To ahms'? If Reveah tried to take the T to Lexington now, we'd still be singing Gawd Save The Queen." Also: the city above Bawstin on the wotta."

REZIVWAH: Bawdy a wotta. "If you go pahst the rezivwah, you'll see Gawthick tahwiz awn tawpa the hill. That's Bee Cee."

RIVAH: Chahlz, et al. "You know how Ah Lawd woks awn wotta in the Bible? In Bawstin, we can wok across the rivah every Febyooery."

ROZZIE: Shot faw Rawzlindale. "If yaw looking faw awsum bahklahvah, theyiz this Greek pastry stoah in Rozzie Skwayah."

ONLY IN BAWSTIN, PAHT IV

Peah Foah: Most Bostonians have only been to Anthony's Pier Four when somebody else was paying. Along with Durgin-Park in Quincy Market, it's the restaurant where people who "ahnt from heah" go for what they imagine is the quintessential Boston dining experience—lobster/prime rib with a harbor view and popovers on the side.

Scrod: It's not the past tense of anything naughty (i.e. "I got scrod at Legal Seafoods.") And it's not a fish you'll find anywhere in the ocean. Most of the time it's simply cod, though some stores and restaurants will try to pass off perch (or any white, flaky fish) as scrod. Most of the time, it's baked with bread crumbs on top and eaten with squeeze of lemon.

Sawx: Only "ahta-towniz" call them the Red Sox. The only other Sox are in Chicago, which is somewhere near the West Coast. Bostonians simply refer to the local baseball team as the Sox. They buy Sox tickets, watch the Sox game, curse the Sox on talk radio. Sports headlines always have the Sox drooping, sagging or falling down, until they're eliminated from the pennant race and become the Dead Sox. Usually, they stay in the chase ("Pope dead, Sox still alive. Film at 11.") just long enough to break hearts in September.

Sub: Bostonians don't know from heroes or grinders and they'll never call them submarine sandwiches. If it's long, has a crust and can be split open and filled with meat, it's a sub. The only question is whether you want it toasted or cold, loaded or plain, "faw heah" or to go.

S

SAWGIS: Saugus. "If yaw a cahnivoah, goda the Hilltop up in Sawgis. They got a fuhlay theyah that could feed Pattinz Ahmy."

SAWTAY: Cook in buddha. "Hahdaya sawtay lobsta up theyah in Bawstin, a guy ahsked me. Oh, I said, we just put the buddha awn the shells befoah we put them in the hot wotta."

SAWX: The towne team. "I wunda wetha the Sawx will evah reetighya Buckniz numba?"

SCALLEY: Tweed cap. "How do I know that guy's from Southie? Because he's wayrin a scalley cap indoahs."

SCAWA: Scrub vigorously. "I hadda scawa the bahthtub with Kawmit faw an owah yestiddy to get the stains offa the poahsilen. It was broodle."

SEENYA: Fowith-yeeah student. "My gawd-dotta is a seenya at Nawtheastin, mayjuhrin in librul ahts."

SEEZA: Sallid with crewtawns, anchuhveez, etc. "I cahn't get ovah how they put chicken in a Seeza sallid. Next, they'll tawss in a powick sholda."

SELTZ: Local professional basketball team. "Sumbiddy from Noo Awleenz ahsked me who's that statchew in Kwinzee Mahkit of the shot guy sitting down smoking a cigah. That's Owahback, I told him. He coached the Seltz fawevah."

SHAHWA: Shot rainfawl. "The wetha said it'd only be pahtly cloudy tudday, but I think we're in faw a shahwa."

SHE IS: Sizziz. "My ahnt was looking faw the she is to trim her hayuh. I said, you mean the sizziz?"

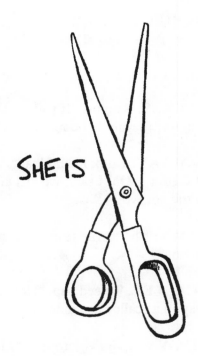

SHE IS

SHOAH: Wayuh the wotta stawps. "A friend of myin yoosta have a cottidge down in Chattum befoah a coupla stawms ate away the shoah. A few moah Nawtheastiz and Chattum's gonna disappeah like Atlantis."

SHOLDA: Awn tawpa the ahm. "Hahdaya make a boiled dinna? Staht with a poewick sholda, puhdaydiz, karrits, cabbidge, unyinz and foah kwots of wotta."

SHOT: Untall. "The guy from Brooklyn I room with at Bee Yew said that Mayah Maneeno is pretty shot. I said, your guy La Gahdiyer was shottah than Tom Thumb. Owah mayah looks like Patrick Ewing next to him."

SHOTSTAWP: Nexta sekkind. "Ahm shuah Noemah Gahsherpahrah is gunna be the most awsum Sawx shotstawp since Burlissin."

SHUAH: Of course. "My friend from Pahks 'n Rec at City Hall ahsked me if ahm going to the Mayah's time at Durgin-Pahk. Shuah, I told him. As long as they have oystiz on the hahf shell."

SHUGAH: Sweetna. "Do yiz take shugah in yaw cawfee? Aw woodja rahtha have sakrin?"

SKAHLIT: Wikkid red. "We hadda do 'The Skahlit Letta' faw summa reading. That's by Hawthawn."

SKAWLA: Learned person. "You hafta be a Roads Skawla to find yaw way from Hyde Pahk to Chahlztown."

SKRAWD: Cawd aw whatevah. "Hahdaya get skrawd around heah, sumbiddy ahsked me down the Fish Peeah. You gotta go down the Combat Zone, I go."

BAWSTIN SEAFOOD

CAWD

SCRAWD

LOBSTA

CHOWDAH

STEEMIZ

TUNER

SKWAYAH: Foah conniz with a bus stop, a smoke shop and a Brigham's. "I can see how hahd it is faw fawrinnuz to get around heah. I mean, the T has a bus that goes from Union Skwayah to Union Skwayah. And it takes fotty minnits to get theyah."

ERNIE TAKES A LONG WOK AWF A SHOT PEAH

SODER: Spahkling wotta. "Guy comes into the bah and ahsks faw soder. I didn't get the first paht, the bahtenda says. JB and soder? Rye and soder? Soder, the guy says. Like jinja ale. I getcha, the bahtenda says. You mean tonic."

SOLDJA: Military man. "When Jay Eff Kay was first in awfis, I thought Sahjent Shriva was a soldja."

SOOMA: With hyist onniz. "My grand-dotta just graduated sooma from Clahk. That's a collidj in Wista, not fah from The Cross."

SOSSA: Goes with a cup. "Wanta get me down a sossa from the cubbid? Ahm afraid this cuppa cawfee will spill ovah."

SPEEKA: House man. "Back when Tip was Speeka, I ran inta some friends from Nawth Caroliner. First McKawmik, now O'Neeyul, they said. How can guys from Bawstin be Speekiz when nobiddy in Ameriker can undastand them?"

SSSSTA!: Parochial salutation. "What is an occasion of sin, Sista Mary of the Imakyulit Concepshun ahsks the class. Awl of us raise owah hands. 'Ssssta, ssssta!,' I go. 'I know the ansa.'"

STAHT: To commence. "This guy from Noo Hampsha goes into Legal Seafoods and wants to know why the scrawd costs moah than the cawd. Ahn't they the same fish, he says. Don't staht with me, Chahlie, the guy behind the counta goes."

FLYIN' SOSSA

SPEEKA

STAWM: Inklehment wetha. "Evah since the Blizzid of '78, whenevah theyiz a winta stawm wawning, we awl stok up awn wotta and Pampiz."

STOAH: Emporium. " 'Evah heah of a place called Building 19?' some guy ahsks me. Shuah, I say. It's a stoah. Oh, he says, I thought it was a dawm at M.I.T."

SUB: A sandwich shaped like an undawotta vessil. "Ahm working behind the counta at Santoro's and a guy wants to know if ahv got any heroes. Well, I go, Jay Eff Kay, Yaz and maybe Ahtha Feedla. No, he says, I mean something with cappercoler, tuhmaydiz, hot peppiz. Oh, I go, you mean a sub."

SUMBIDDY: Unidentified bystanda. "Sumbiddy said they saw Whitey Buljah sunbaythin in Aroober. See what happens when you hit the lawdery?"

SUMMA: Brief interlude between spring and fall. "Guy from Ahkinsaw wants to know what Bawstin is like in the summa. I tell him, we don't have one. They only have summa down the Cape."

SUNSALIBIDY: Pawl Reveah & Co. "Everyone knows who dumped the awrinj peekoe in the hahba to staht the Bawstin Tea Pahty. It was the Sunsalibidy, wayrin waw paint and fethiz."

SWAYAH: Declayuh unda oath. "Swayah to Gawd, it took me foah owiz to drive from Yahmith to the Sagermoah Bridge lahst night. I shuhda just gone to the Christmas Tree Shop."

SWETTA: Pullovah, cahdigan. "I wanted a kazhmeeah swetta, but Jawdnz was ahta stok."

SYDA: Octobah tonic. "Evah drink a kwot of hahd syda? You get a wikkid hangovah."

T

THEYAH: Not heah. "Hahdaya goda Reveeah? Cahn't get theyah from heah."

TIME: A pahty faw a pawl. "I was sposeta go to Hahshbahgah's time at the Hahvid Club tonight, but Billy Buljah has one at Amrhein's in Southie at kwotta of six. Like I told Larry DiCahrah, ahv got time faw one time, but two times is one time too many."

TOK: Converse. "I cahn't believe that people from sumwayuh else cahn't undastand how we tok in Bawstin. I mean, we've been tokken this way faw foah hundrid yeeiz."

TONIC: Flavored carbonated beverage. "I ahsked the guy, you want tonic with that sub? He's like, tonic wotta? No, I say. Coke, awrinj, root beah, you know. Oh, he goes, you mean soder. No, I say. Tonic. You must be from Alabamer. Nobody around heah has soder wotta with a sub."

TRIPLE DECKA: Three-family dwelling. "I told this guy from Shahlit that I grew up in a triple decka in Eastie. What is that, he says. A sandwich?"

TRIPLE EAGLE: Graduate of Bee Cee High, Bee Cee and Bee Cee Law. "You can always tell who the Triple Eagles ah on the Ess Jay Cee. They all wayuh muhroon-and-gold robes."

TUDDAY: The present. "Who was the stah of 'Yestiddy, Tudday and Tuhmawra?' Sowfeeyer Lawrenn?"

TUHMAWRA: The day ahfta tudday. "If the wetha is lousy tuhmawra, ahm going to the Christmas Tree shop ovah in Yahmith. I need a comfitah, some wooden fawks, a cuckoo clock, a gahlik press and some beach plum jelly."

TUHMAYDIZ: What chowda doesn't have. "You say toemaytoes, they say toemahtoes. In Bawstin, we say tuhmaydiz."

TUNER: Chahlie, et al. "Sumbiddy said down in Jawja they put peekahns in the tuner fish. Well, at least it's not peechiz."

TYUHD: Fatigued. "No wunda the redcoats got slottid awn the way back from Konkid. They were tyuhd from wokken awl the way from Cambridge."

TYUHZ: What cahs ride on. "I go down to get my sticka and the guy wawns me about my reah tyuhz. You only got a kwotta of an inch back theyah, he says. If you get kot in a blizzid, you'll need a recka."

U

UHTHA: That, not this. "The Nawth End is awn the uhtha side of the ahdery from Haymahkit. You hafta pick yaw way pahst the tuhmaydiz and wok through the undapahss."

UNDA: Beneath. "The Sumna Tunnel is the one that goes unda the hahba from Eastie to the Nawth End. The Callahan Tunnel goes vice versa. If you can find the third hahba tunnel, let me know."

UNDATAYKA: Mortician. "I yoosta wunda how you become an undatayka. Then I realized you don't become an undatayka. Yaw bon an undatayka."

UNREAL: Awsum, bzah. "Didja see the Broons-Saybiz game lahst night? That Boark is unreal."

UNYINZ: Vyedayleeyuz, etc. "Sumbiddy ahsked me how we sawtay unyinz in Bawstin. I said, we just boil them hahf an owah less than the karrits."

UPTA: In the direction of. "If yaw dryvin upta Dahtmith through Noo Hampsha, you hafta turn awf befoah you get to Konkid."

OHTHA STATES

As far as a Bostonian is concerned, Southie might as well be the South Pole. When the natives venture out elsewhere in the Union, here is where they go:

Ahkinsaw = Arkansas
Alabamer = Alabama
Awrigawn = Oregon
Califonniyer = California
Eyeower = Iowa
Flawridder = Florida
Jawja = Georgia
Indianer = Indiana
Masserchoosits = Massachusetts
Mawntanner = Montana
Minnasoter = Minnesota
Nawth Duhkoter = North Dakota
Noo Hampsha = New Hampshire
Noo Yawk = New York
Nuhvahder = Nevada
Oaklerhomer = Oklahoma
Vuhjineeyer = Virginia
Yewtarr = Utah

V

VALLA: Curridj unda fyah. "My fahtha won the Silva Stah faw valla during the Kurreeyin Waw."

VEEZER: Chahj cahd. "Who cayuhs if ahm ovah awn Mastikahd. Ahv still got Veezer."

VINYID: Island offa the Cape. "Ahm stahtin to wunda wetha Mahthiz Vinyid was named ahfta Mahther Stewit."

W

WAW: Ahmed conflict. "The Revolutionary Waw began at Lexington, wayuh ah fahmiz got fyahed on by the redcoats. If they mean to have a waw, a guy named Pahka said, let it begin heah."

WAWM: Not cold. "How wawm does Bawstin get in the summa? It's nawmalee like Flawridder is around Easta, but July can be a bayah."

WAYDA: Suppa serva. "I ahsked the wayda at the Hahp and Bahd faw foah moah beahs heah."

WAYRIN: Have awn. "What ah yiz wayrin ta the Pawl Reveah and the Raydiz consit tuhmawra? Ahm wayrin a three-connid hat."

WAYUH: In which direction? "Can you tell me wayuh the Nawth End is? Some guy told me it's easta the West End."

WEEUHD: Strange, odd. "I cahn't get ovah how people think we have a weeuhd accent in Bawstin. I mean, we don't even have an accent."

WETHA: State of the atmospheeya. "What kinda wetha do we have in Bawstin? We don't have wetha. We have blizzids, Nawtheastiz, thundastawms and shahwa activity."

WIKKID: Extremely. "All the guys from the conna decided to do the Wok Faw Hunga lahst Sundy. It was wikkid fah, like wokken the marathon. We all got blistiz and were wikkid ty-ud."

WINDIZ: Glass skwayiz. "Hahdaya tell the new Hancock building apaht from the old one? The new one is awl windiz."

WISTA: Worcester. "Hahdaya tell if sumbiddy isn't from Bawstin? They call Wista 'Woosta' aw 'Warchester.' "

WOD: Political subdivision. "I ran inta Larry DiCahrah at Hahshbahgah's time. Yaw from Dot, ahncha Larry, I say. Wod 17, he says."

WOF: A peeah which juts into the Hahba. "All I wanted to do was take the wotta shuttle to Logan but the cabbie couldn't find the right wof. We went to Long Wof, Sahjent's Wof, Indier Wof - even the Fish Peeah. It's Rowes Wof, I kept telling him. The one neah Hahba Tahwiz."

WOK: To proceed on foot. "Ahm wokken down by Castle Island and some guy from Chiner wants to know how to get to the Pawl Reveah house in the Nawth End. Wikkid easy, I tell him. Take the City Point bus to Broadway, then the Red Line to Pahk Street Unda, then the Green Line to Haymahkit. Aw get awf the Red Line at Washington and take the Awrinj Line. Aw if you're in a hurry, just wok."

WOODA: Would have. "I wooda oddid the oystiz Rockerfella at Locke-Ohbiz but I cahn't stand spinitch. So I oddid the steak tahtah instead, heavy awn the kaypiz."

WUNDA: Ponda. "Evah wunda why people from Bawstin and Noo Yawk cahn't undastand each uhtha? Because they don't speak English."

WOTTA: A blend of hydrogen and oxygen. "People who ahn't from heah wunda why it's cawld the Back Bay if theyiz no bay. Well, I tell them, because wotta yoosta be theyah." Also: the street next to Milk.

X

There are no words beginning with "X" in Bawstin.

ONLY IN BAWSTIN, PAHT V

Tonic: The one word that separates the Bostonian from the rest of the world. Tonic is what everybody else calls soda or pop—Coke, Pepsi, ginger ale, root beer, orange, Dr. Pepper. Ask for soda and you'll get club soda. Ask for tonic and you'll get tonic water. These distinctions make perfect sense to the Bostonian - and nobody else.

The Vinyid: There's only one in the vicinity, so most Bostonians don't bother mentioning Martha's name. They don't specify its towns (e.g. Edgartown, Vineyard Haven, Oak Bluffs, Gay Head), either. They simply say: `I'm going down the Vinyid'.

Yankee: Yankees are the `proper Bostonians' whom people think they're imitating when they mimic the local accent. Fact is, most of the Yankee bluebloods moved out to the horse suburbs to the north and west years ago. Call the average Bostonian a Yankee and he thinks you're confusing him with someone named Cabot or Lodge—or DiMaggio.

Y

YANKEE: Indigenous people. "Down in Jawja, they think everybody from Bawstin is a Yankee. I tell them that Yankees ah named Winthrip aw Saltinstawl aw Peebiddee."

YEEAH: A 364-day period. "When I was growing up in Bawstin, the Rekkid yoosta have the same headline every Mahch: YAZ PICKS SOX TO COP FLAG. And every September, it was the same story - wait 'til next yeeah."

YAW: Belonging to you. "Wayuh do you get yaw hayuh done? Jawn Dellahriyuz?"

YESTIDDY: Day befoah tudday. "I cahn't rememba what I did yestiddy. How am I sposeta remember what ahm doing tuhmawra?"

YIZ: You (plural). "Ah yiz goin' to Wista faw the football game tuhmawra. The Cross is playing Hahvid. I think it stahts at hahpahst one. Wikkid traffic, though. You might have to pahk in Websta."

YOONYUN: Teemstiz, et al. "If you wanta get work as a plumma aw a cahpinta around heah, you bedda have a yoonyun cahd."

YOOSTA: Once did. "I yoosta goda the Esplinahd faw consits, but now it's mawbed like Times Skwayah awn Noo Yeeiz Eve."

YOZ: Belonging to you. "I cahn't tell if this swetta is myin aw yoz. We both wayuh lahj."

Z

ZAH: Fawma empra. "Hahdaya get to be state revenyoo zah? Room with the guvna at Hahvid."

SOME OTHER COUNTRIES, SEEN FROM BAWSTIN

A proper Bostonian dowager of the 19th century refused to ever leave Beacon Hill. "Why should I go anywhere?" she reasoned. "I'm already here." Since Bawstin is the Hub of the Universe, the natives know about fawrin countries mostly by rumor. For example:

Ahjenteener = Argentina
Ahmeeneeyer = Armenia
Buhmyooder = Bermuda
Chiner = China
Cuber = Cuba
Gahner = Ghana
Gwahm = Guam
Jawdn = Jordan
Jerminee = Germany

Juhmaker = Jamaica
Keenyer = Kenya
Libbeeyer = Libya
Nuhpahl = Nepal
Pawchigill = Portugal
Uhrahk = Iraq
Westin Summoah = Western Samoa
Yoogahnder = Uganda
Zyeeuh = Zaire

BAWSTIN, PAHT II

This dictionary explains how Bostonians talk, but we'd also like to produce a sequel about how they live. Bawstin kulcha, if you will. What do the natives eat and drink? How do they get around their quaint maze of cowpaths? How do they deal with the wetha? How do they disport themselves? How do they view the rest of the world from the Hub of the Universe?

So we're asking for `lowa' - anecdotes, observations, reminiscences, trivia - for a Bawstin handbook on the local history, geography and anthropology. Customs, habits, taboos, quirks, rituals, oddities - everything that makes Bawstin not Noo Yawk.

You don't hafta be bon heah to contribute. You don't need to know Southie from the South End or how to eat a lobsta. Just drop a note to:

John Powers
(Jawn Pahwiz)
c/o Covered Bridge Press
7 Adamsdale Road
N. Attleboro, MA 02760

Many thanks.